Try This At Home!

Amazing Bike Tricks

Ellen Labrecque

Raintree

Raintree is an imprint of Capstone Global Library Limited, a company incorporated in England and Wales having its registered office at 7 Pilgrim Street, London, EC4V 6LB – Registered company number: 6695582

To contact Raintree please phone 0845 6044371, fax + 44 (0) 1865 312263, or email myorders@ raintreepublishers.co.uk. Customers from outside the UK please telephone +44 1865 312262.

Text © Capstone Global Library Limited 2013
First published in hardback in 2013
Paperback edition first published in 2014
The moral rights of the proprietor have been asserted.

Edited by Rebecca Rissman, Daniel Nunn, and Adrian Vigliano
Designed by Cynthia Della-Rovere
Picture research by Elizabeth Alexander
Production by Alison Parsons
Originated by Capstone Global Library Ltd
Printed and bound in China by China Translation and Printing Services Ltd

ISBN 978 1 406 25099 2 (hardback)
16 15 14 13 12
10 9 8 7 6 5 4 3 2 1

ISBN 978 1 406 25106 7 (paperback)
17 16 15 14
10 9 8 7 6 5 4 3 2

British Library Cataloguing in Publication Data
Labrecque, Ellen.
Amazing bike tricks. -- (Try this at home!)
796.6-dc23
A full catalogue record for this book is available from the British Library.

Acknowledgements
We would like to thank the following for permission to reproduce photographs: Alamy p. 7 (© A. T. Willett); © Capstone Publishers pp. 8, 9, 10, 11 t, 11 b, 12 b, 12 t, 13 t, 13 b, 14, 15 t, 15 b, 16, 17 t, 17 b, 18 t, 18 b, 19 t, 19 b, 20 t, 20 b, 21 t, 21 b, 22, 23 t, 23 b, 24, 25, 26 t, 26 b, 27, 28, 29 (Karon Dubke); Shutterstock p. 6 (© Attl Tibor); SuperStock pp. 4 (© Transtock), 5 (© Corbis). Design features reproduced with the permission of istockphoto (© Felix Alim); Shutterstock (© Snow Coyote), (© Gines Valera Marin), (© Merve Poray), (© Nicemonkey), (© Merve Poray).

Cover photograph of a BMX biker performing tricks reproduced with permission of Corbis (© Nice One Productions).

Every effort has been made to contact copyright holders of material reproduced in this book. Any omissions will be rectified in subsequent printings if notice is given to the publisher.

Contents

Some words are shown in bold, **like this**. You can find out what they mean by looking in the Glossary.

What are bike tricks?

Most children learn to ride a bike. But most children don't learn how to do amazing tricks while riding. With lots of practice and some guts, you can pull off some of the coolest bike tricks around!

By the end of this book, you'll even learn some of those rad moves you see on television and in **BMX** magazines. They will be sure to amaze your friends. So let's fly, or ... ride!

Be safe!

First, take your bike to the local bike shop and get it tuned up. Make sure the brakes, chain, and pedals all work. A bike **mechanic** can also put **stunt pegs** on your bike, which are necessary for a lot of tricks.

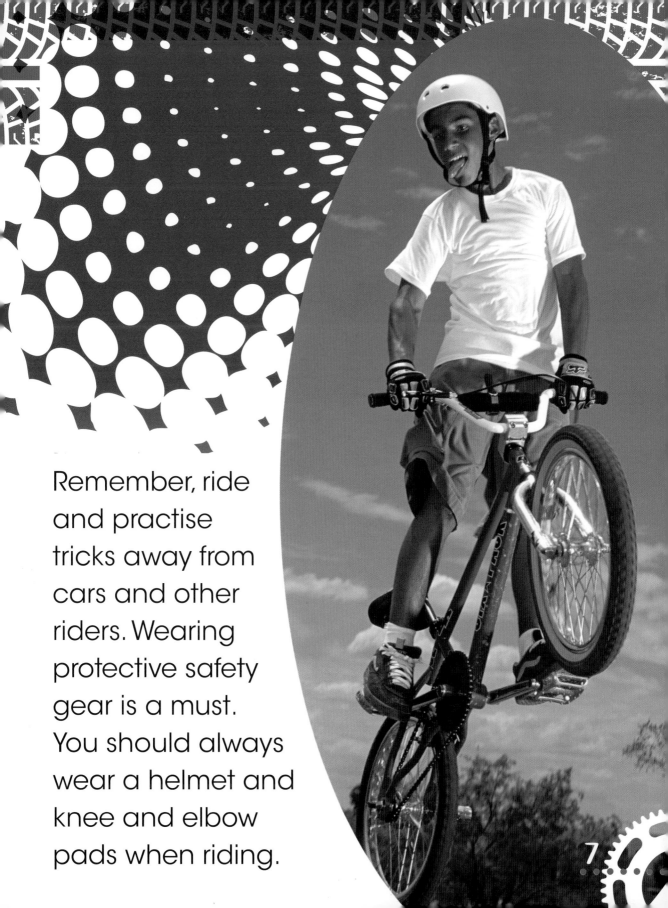

Remember, ride and practise tricks away from cars and other riders. Wearing protective safety gear is a must. You should always wear a helmet and knee and elbow pads when riding.

Strike a pose

Before trying tricks, you need to get used to one important move: the step over.

STEP 1

Ride your bike normally, then take one foot off the pedal and bring that leg over the bike. Both legs will end up on the same side of the bike. Make sure you keep your weight even and your standing leg slightly bent.

When you are ready to pedal again, throw your leg back to its correct pedal. Put weight onto both feet and pedal forwards.

Endo

STEP 1

While riding your bike slowly, apply your front brakes.

Insider tip:

Always start at an easy level and work your way up.

Push forward on the handlebars, and your weight should shift forward. Your knees should be bent, and your head should be over the front tyre. Your back tyre will fly into the air. Keep gripping the front brakes to stay up in the air.

When you are ready to finish the trick, lean back and gently let the back tyre fall onto the ground.

Front hop

STEP 1

Ride slowly, then apply the front brakes sharply. Push your arms forward and shift your weight forward, so that your back wheel goes up.

STEP 2

When your back wheel goes up, keep your arms locked.

STEP 3 Apply pressure on your pedals and lift up your handlebars at the same time. Your bike will do a hop.

When done hopping, let go of the brakes and lean back into your ride. **STEP 4**

Insider tip:

Start with doing just two hops at first, and build your way up to more.

13

Manual

STEP 1

Balancing on your back wheel while rolling is called a manual. First, pedal at an easy speed. Next, pull up and back on your handlebars and shift your weight behind your seat.

Insider tip:

The trick is to find the right balancing point so you don't fall backwards.

14

Keep your balance by tugging on the handlebars and gently squeezing your rear hand brake.

STEP **3**

Stay up and balanced as long as you can. Then, set the front wheel down gently and ride away.

How to ride fakie

STEP 1

Riding **fakie** is riding backwards. Find a ramp that you can ride down. Pedal up the ramp or **incline**.

Insider tip:

Once you stop pedalling up the hill, the bike will naturally start backing down.

STEP 2

When you get high enough to roll back, stop pedalling and allow yourself to go backwards.

STEP 3

Don't hunch over the handlebars. Stay up and keep your weight balanced. This will allow you to ride straight out.

17

Bunny hop

Level of difficulty: Easy

STEP 1

The bunny hop is a way to get air without a ramp. While you are riding forwards, pull up on your handlebars.

STEP 2

Straighten your legs to apply pressure against your pedals.

Pull the rear end up using your body, especially your legs. Once both wheels are off the ground, tuck your knees to level the bike.

STEP 4

Land on both wheels at the same time.

Bar spin

Level of difficulty: Medium

This trick is definitely impressive. Roll towards a ramp. At the top, pull up on the handlebars to lift the front end of your bike.

STEP **1**

STEP **2**

When you're in the air, release one hand and use the other to spin the handlebars towards you.

STEP 3

Catch the bars after they go around a full **rotation**.

STEP 4

Then set the front wheel down and ride on.

Insider tip:

Practise catching the bars by pressing your rear wheel against a wall to keep your bike steady. Pull up the front end and spin the bar over and over.

Drop in

Level of difficulty:
Medium

STEP **1**

When you go to drop in, lift your front wheel just a bit to help clear the top of the ramp.

Insider tip:

Remember to turn your wheel in the direction you want to go when dropping in.

STEP 2

Come into the **half-pipe** on an angle instead of straight down. This will make the drop seem less steep.

STEP 3

Once you get over the top, look straight ahead and ride right out.

Can can

The can can is a hard aerial trick. Make sure you are padded from head to toe before trying this one. Find a jump that you are comfortable riding on. Pedal hard to get a good amount of speed.

STEP 1

24

When you hit the jump, lift your right foot off the pedal as soon as the bike leaves the jump.

Move the right leg over the **tube** or middle bar, so that you have both feet on the same side. Leave your left foot on the pedal.

Your right foot should point to the left side of your body.

STEP **4**

Move your right foot back onto its pedal.

26

Spot your landing and hit it with both tyres landing at the same time.

Insider tip:

Practise first with just taking your foot off the pedal in the air without lifting it over the bar.

Be stylish!

Think you have mastered these bike tricks? Excellent! You also want to look cool while you do them, right? Here are some tips on how to look stylish while pulling off these moves.

1. Master the basics – don't try the hardest tricks first.
2. The longer you can hold a trick, the cooler it looks.

3. Do the trick with **confidence**.

4. Put safety first. Nobody looks cool in the back of an ambulance.

5. Have fun and don't forget to smile – that will be your coolest look of all.

Glossary

BMX bicycle racing on a dirt track

confidence belief in yourself and your abilities

fakie ride backwards

half-pipe U-shaped ramp used by riders to do tricks

incline upward slope

mechanic person skilled in fixing bikes

rotation turn in a circular motion. A full rotation forms a complete circle.

stunt pegs short tubes attached to a bike that riders can use to perform tricks

tube middle bar on a bike

Find out more

Books

BMX and Mountain Biking (World Sports Guide), Paul Mason (A & C Black, 2010)

BMX Riding Skills: The Guide to Flatland Tricks, Shek Hon (Firefly Books, 2010)

Street Sports: Freestyle BMX (Radar), Isabel Thomas (Wayland, 2011)

Websites

bmx.transworld.net/tag/magazine
A site to browse all the latest BMX news.

espn.go.com/action
A great site to read about all action sports, especially BMX.

www.vitalbmx.com
Tagged as the number one BMX website.

Index